SIMPLE PARENTING SKILLS IN MINUTES

Create a happy, loving relationship with your child

BY

GRAINNE BRADY

WWW.CHILDKNOWHOW.COM

Copyright © 2018 Grainne Brady

All rights reserved. No part of this publication may be reproduced, distributed, or transmitted in any form or by any means, including photocopying, recording, or other electronic or mechanical methods, without the prior written permission of the author, except in the case of brief quotations embodied in critical reviews and certain other non-commercial uses permitted by copyright law. For permission requests, contact the author at the address below.

Printed by   CreateSpace,

An Amazon.com Company

Available from Amazon.com, CreateSpace.com, and other retail outlets First Printing, 2018

ISBN 978-1-9999184-0-8

Publishing Grainne Brady www.childknowhow.com

ABOUT THE AUTHOR

Grainne Brady was born in County Roscommon, Ireland. She has an M.A. in Practice Based Play Therapy and thirty five years' experience working with children and parents. Her interest in childcare began with the birth of her eldest daughter, Jasmine. She realised that there was more to rearing children than ensuring they were fed, warm and dry. This began the journey of understanding the emotional needs of children.

She started off studying Maria Montessori, loving the theory behind the method so she became a Montessori teacher. She later studied Child Development, High Scope and finally became a Play Therapist. She taught child development and parenting to parents, grandparents and childcare workers over a twenty year period up to post graduate level. She worked in many childcare facilities supporting parents and children. In later years, she worked as a Play Therapist and a Play Therapy supervisor.

Throughout her career working with children she attended numerous, continuous, professional development programmes and read all she could on the subject.

Over those thirty five years, she accumulated different techniques of working more positively with her own children and with other children in various childcare settings.

ACKNOWLEDGEMENTS

I dedicate this book to my mother Maud

I would like to acknowledge my daughters, Jasmine and Erica, without whom I would not have written this book;

PJ, Geraldine, Frances, Sue and Mary, for their assistance in completing this book.

I would like to thank my sisters Deirdre and Siobhan for their input. I acknowledge my brothers, sisters and friends for their lifelong love, friendship and support.

Illustrations by
Mary Smyth
behance.net/marysmyth

Table of Contents

Introduction	1
Part 1	5
1 The Needs of Children	5
2 Unconditional Love	7
3 Helping Your Child Control Emotions	9
4 The Parent as Teacher	11
5 Establishing Routine	14
6 A Hundred Hugs a Day	16
7 Keeping Your Child Safe	19
8 House Rules	21
9 Children Need Responsibility	23
10 Listening for Feelings	25
11 Listening for Facts	28
12 Spending Time with Your Child	30
13 Being in Your Child's Game	32
14 Acknowledge Effort	35
15 Healthy Eating	37
16 Teach Requesting	40
17 Children Learn by Doing	42

18	Teach Feeling Language	45
19	Giving Your Child Attention	47
20	Learning Decision Making	49
21	Planning as a Family	52
22	Community Involvement	54
23	Parent Self-Care	56

Part 2		58
24	Your Child is Separate from Your Child's Behaviour	58
25	Misbehaving and What the Child Gains	60
26	Natural Consequences	62
27	Logical Consequences	64
28	Problem Solving With the Young Child	67
29	Problem Solving for the Older Child	73
30	When and….Then	79
31	Feeling.. Limit.. Another Action	81
32	Requesting a Change of Behaviour from Your Child	83
33	Children's Asking Styles	85
34	'Time Out'	88
35	Self-Defence Parenting	90
36	Building Self-Esteem Tips.	93
37	Reducing Conflict at Home	97
Part 3		101

Difficulties Experienced by Parents 101

Conclusion 111

Introduction

This book is a very simple, short guide full of techniques and tips to help parents create closer relationships with their children. I want this book to help families worldwide to create happy, harmonious, connected relationships with very strong bonds. I would like it to help families to enjoy each other, love doing things together and love hanging out with each other.

In this book you will mainly find a technique in every section that will help you support your child's development. Each technique stands alone. Put all the techniques together and a parenting framework is created. The techniques can be applied to any age. The younger the child is when you start using the book, the closer your relationship will be with your child.

The techniques in this book are what I have found effective when rearing my children and when working with other children. I am very aware of the difficulties of raising children. The help that parents need when they need it, is not always readily available. Parents are very busy people, so the idea of this book is to teach techniques that can be quickly learned and put to use.

Family life was changing at a rapid rate when I was rearing my children and is still evolving at great speed. The difficulties rearing a family had changed and I quickly realised I did not have the skills to create a harmonious, happy family life.

I did every parenting programme I could, to learn better ways of working with my children. I needed help so I became a 'guinea pig', trying out techniques from psychologists, social workers and every other 'expert' in the business. I did not care I needed help. I read every parenting book, child development book and gradually built up a repertoire of techniques I have used successfully over the years. The techniques I have included in this book are the ones that worked. Many more techniques were discarded after trying them, without success.

I have created this book as a 'dip in and dip out' guide for parents to build up skills quickly. It is meant to be a 'read and run' book. It is an acknowledgement of the very difficult job parents do raising children.

In my opinion, there is nothing more important than rearing the next generation. I think it is totally undervalued and rarely given the respect it deserves.

Part One of the book focuses on positive ways of working with children to build good relationships. It starts off outlining the basic needs of children. This section covers building your child's self-esteem, developing a positive sense of self and ways of creating a great relationship between you and your child, avoiding difficulties.

Part Two includes quick techniques for you to use when dealing with your child's difficult behaviour. At different times in a child's life there are pivotal changes, both developmentally and in family life. As a child grows, their needs change and parents often struggle with the child's behaviour at these times. Parents, especially with their first child, are often slow to see these changes and so struggle to adapt to the new status quo with their child. I believe when a child exhibits difficult behaviour, the child is sending out a loud message saying 'something is not right in my world'.

Part Three has the most frequently asked questions from parents. The answers refer the reader back to the relevant section in the book to help solve their difficulty.

Each section has a very simple, short structure. The book is written for non-readers and busy parents primarily. It can be used by child care providers, family agencies, teachers, child care professionals and anyone with responsibility for children. There is a general description of the technique and the reason for using it. It is followed by a number of examples, the message the child receives and some tips. Sometimes I have used 'they', 'their' or 'them' in examples for convenience. The examples apply to both genders equally.

Part 1

1 The Needs of Children

Children need a number of basic things in their lives to develop and grow.

1.   They need nutritious food to grow into healthy adults.
2.   They need a safe, secure place to live, free from attack or the threat of attack - which means free from being slapped by adults or older children. They need to be free of the threat of injury, kept safe from harm and every kind of abuse.

3.   Children need routine to give their lives some kind of order, following some kind of a daily pattern. This helps them to predict their day.

4.   They need love and acceptance from the adults around them. They need to be loved unconditionally for themselves, firstly by their parents, siblings and close family. They later need friends and to practice building relationships. The strength of their early relationships decides the strength of all of their later life relationships.

They need opportunities to learn about the world around them. They need materials, either toys or real things to explore the world into which they have been born. They need to be taught to do everything for themselves and then given appropriate responsibility to become fully functioning. They need role models to watch and copy, adults that take time to be with them, to teach them, teach them again and again patiently. This book focusses on simple ways of meeting the child's needs.

2 Unconditional Love

Children need to feel loved and accepted for themselves by the people around them, especially their parents or main carers. Showing your child love is important. Telling your child you love them exactly as they are, regularly, helps them to feel loved.

Children who feel loved and accepted for themselves grow up with confidence and self-esteem. They are born into the world helpless. They adapt to life around them, which they know nothing about. They look to you, the parent or primary carer for love, care and guidance.

They need to be unconditionally loved. You need to communicate your love to your child in all your actions. The child needs to know that what they think and say is important to you.

You need to communicate that you enjoy being with your child, that you love hanging out with them, playing with them, talking to them. You must get across the message that no matter what their behaviour is like, you love and accept them anyway. Separating your child's behaviour from your child helps them know that they are loved no matter what happens.

Example 1
"John, I love you exactly as you are. You are great fun to be around. Come over here so I can give you a big hug."

Example 2
"Let me finish what I am doing so that I can sit and listen carefully to what you have to say. It is important for me to hear what you're saying."

Example 3
"I really enjoy chatting with you when you come in from school. I really love to hear all your news."

The Message the Child Receives
My mum/dad loves me, I am important, what I do is important

Tip
Never compare your children with each other or with children outside the family. It belittles them and sets up competitiveness and hostility between them.

3 Helping Your Child Control Emotions

When children are young they do not know how to deal with frustrations that arise. The young child is egocentric, meaning that they think their needs are the only needs to be satisfied. They do not know that you and everyone else has feelings and needs too. They only learn that through life experience over time.

Example 1
John, aged two wants the toy his older brother Pat has. John grabs the toy out of Pat's hand, hitting him with the toy. Pat takes it right back off him and John starts crying loudly. All John knows is that he wants that toy now. The parent comforts John calmly and lovingly, telling him he can have the toy when Pat is finished with it. Pat had the toy first and he is playing with it. In this way John learns that Pat has rights too. John has to wait until Pat is finished and then he can have a turn.

Example 2
Leah, aged three, bites Jack, when he will not give her a piece of his chocolate. She has already finished hers and they both start crying. The parent comforts both children - Jack because he is

hurt and Leah because she is dealing with her frustration of not getting what she wants, when she wants it. The parent explains that she is not allowed to bite and that she has eaten her own chocolate and that the chocolate that Jack is eating is his.

Example 3

Amira wants to go outside even though she has a cold and it is raining. She cries and shouts to go out. Her mother soothes her and explains to her that it is cold and raining outside and she cannot go out because she is sick. Amira is comforted by her mum.

The Message the Child Receives

I can't do that, there is a reason and it's alright because my parent still loves me.

Tip

It is crucial for young children to have this early soothing experience from their parents, to help them deal with their frustrations so that they can learn to self-soothe when later faced with other difficulties.

4 The Parent as Teacher

Never do for your child what your child is able to do for themselves.
"I'll do it myself," is a common statement from young children. They want to do everything for themselves. By taking the time to teach your child valuable life skills you do them a great service, allowing them to grow in self-esteem and self-confidence so they can become capable, independent adults.

How to:
Teach your child how to do everything from the day they are able. Start by showing them how to do a task they are interested in. As they get older, teach them what they want to know - a young child wants to learn to tie their shoelaces while an older child wants to learn to cook or use the washing machine. However, always keep in mind safety for their age.

Example 1
If your child wants to close their own coat, start with a simple zipper. Show them how to close the zipper with the minimum number of movements and a basic explanation. Allow your child to

attempt the task and do not correct them while they are doing it. If they do something wrong, wait and teach them the task again at another time, again, with the minimum number of movements. Teach your child the same task repeatedly over time until they master the task. Encourage them by pointing out what they have done well.

Example 2

Teach your child to butter their bread with a blunt knife, using only a few movements and clear, concise instructions. Then let them try. If you have a problem with the child digging into the butter, put it into a small container and then give them a turn.

Example 3

If your child wants to wash their own hair, demonstrate how to wash hair. Put the amount of baby shampoo needed into a small bottle for your child to use. Give the small bottle to your child and let them wash their own hair. By doing this you are avoiding stressing about the large bottle of shampoo going down the drain.

The Message the Child Receives
I am trusted, I am able by myself and I am loved.

Tip

When your child has mastered a task do not carry it out for them again. They are able to do it by themselves now. Progress by helping your child with a task that is beyond their ability. Give them only the amount of help that they need to do the task themselves.

5 Establishing Routine

Creating routine in a child's day is all about doing things at certain times of the day. If possible, repeat some of the same things every day. Routine is important for children. It gives them a sense of security in their day. Children need some things to stay the same from one day to another. Some children, for example, those with additional needs, will require more routine to feel safe.

How to:
All families are different and do different things. It does not matter what kind of a routine your family has, as long as there is some routine in the day. It can be as simple as having breakfast, getting dressed, eating dinner and going to bed at a certain time.

Example 1
A week day routine might be getting up in the morning at 8 am, getting dressed, having breakfast, going to school, coming home, doing homework, eating dinner, doing chores, playtime, supper time and going to bed at a certain time.

Example 2
A weekend routine might be getting up at 10am, getting breakfast, getting dressed, watching TV, doing some chores, playtime, lunchtime, family shopping, dinner and quiet time.

Example 3
A holiday routine might be getting up at 10am, having breakfast, getting dressed, tidying their bedroom, going to the playground, having a picnic in the park, returning home, doing the chores, helping to prepare dinner, a little playtime and going to bed time.

The Message the Child Receives
I'm safe and I know what will happen in my day.

Tip
Have at least two things the same every day. A family meal once a day where the family eat together is a good routine to have daily.
A bedtime routine will work for some families.

6 A Hundred Hugs a Day

Hug your child regularly throughout the day. Children need to feel loved and this is a direct way of telling them or showing them. It guarantees positive behaviour in your child. The child is able to focus on growing and developing, not looking for your love and attention. The child grows in self-confidence and self-esteem. The child receives unconditional love.

How to:
Give them a hug in the morning when they get up, a hug when they are going to school, a hug when they come home and a hug before bedtime. Make it a ritual in your house. Add in caring pats on the head throughout the day, a quick hug and let go. There are many ways to let your child know that you love them. Remember to tell them that you love them regularly.

Example 1
Just as your son or daughter is leaving for school, get down to their eye level, give them eye contact and a smile, followed by a big hug and wish them a good day.

Example 2
Say to your child, 'I love you dearly'. Say it regularly and mean it. Include it in your 'Hundred Hugs a Day' ritual.

The Message the Child Receives
I am loved and I am loveable. I am a good person, my parents and the world around me love me.

Tip
Start the ritual when your child is young and carry it on throughout their lives. A child is never too old for a hug or to be told they are loved. Hugs help to release Dopamine, 'the happy chemical' which helps children feel secure and loved. So hug your child lavishly and often.

7 Keeping Your Child Safe

Children do not instinctively know what is safe and what is dangerous, so it is your responsibility as a parent to keep them safe and teach them about the dangers around them.

How to:
Carry out an assessment of the dangers in your home to decide what needs to be done. When your child starts to crawl, look at the possible dangers in the home and remove them.

Use safety equipment like a fireguard and a stair gate. Keep them away from the cooker and the kettle by using guards. Keep medicines and detergents locked away in a high cupboard, out of the reach of children and put locks on drawers with sharp objects, cupboards with chemicals, upstairs windows and doors leading onto the street. Use socket covers for plug sockets. Never leave young children unsupervised or on their own. Never let young children eat unsupervised, there is a risk of choking. Keep small objects out of the reach of young children.

Remove things you value from where your child plays. This will lessen rows between you and your child. Valued ornaments, jewellery, expensive mobile phones and make-up should be removed from where the child can reach them easily.

Example 1
Lock the gate onto the road when your child is playing outside. Young children should always be supervised.

Example 2
Make sure children do not have access to ponds, tubs of water, electric wires or anything else they could drown in or be electrocuted by.

Example 3
Tell children that the stove is hot and will hurt their hand. Explain to children the dangers involved and so teach them what is dangerous and what is not.

The Message the Child Receives
I am safe, protected and loved.

Tip
Do not expect your child to know that the fire burns or a car might hit them if they run onto the road. Child safety is the responsibility of the adult.

8 House Rules

Children feel safe when rules are consistent and they know what they are. If rules constantly change children don't feel secure.

How to:
You the parent needs to work out the rules of the house and tell your child what the rules are. Keep the rules simple and make sure everyone in the house knows them. The rules must stay the same every day, for everybody. Some homes will have more rules than others but you should make as few rules as is necessary to run the home smoothly. For young children use as few rules as possible. Think about the consequences of implementing a rule before you do, because once it's in place there should be no deviating from it. As the parent, you lead the family and must sometimes make decisions that are not popular with your children. Your role is to make decisions that are best for the child and the family, not to placate or be popular with your child.

Examples of rules
Rule 1.   No hurting anybody in the house

Rule 2.No breaking things in the house
Rule 3.No shouting at each other
Rule 4.Bedtime is 8pm

These are basic rules, other rules might be around homework, mealtime, morning time. For simplicity and clarity I put the rules in the negative form rather than in the positive form. Clear understanding of the rules by all is the key.

The Message the Child Receives
I am safe, I know what is expected of me. I know what the rules are.

Tip
The key to success is that rules are consistent every day and do not change even if you are tired or sick. If you say 'no' to a child's request, then 'no' means 'no'. If you have not thought about the request, say 'let me think about it' and then come back with your answer later.

9 Children Need Responsibility

As early in life as possible children need tasks that contribute to the family they belong to. This gives them a sense of belonging in the family and teaches them that their input is important. They learn responsibility and grow in self-confidence. The younger the child has responsibility for family tasks, the better for their growth and development.

How to:
First, write a list of household jobs and ask the children to choose which jobs they would like to take on. Teach your child how to carry out those tasks, then let them do it themselves. Teach the tasks again if they do not succeed. If the child is reluctant to do the task, talk with them to find out what the problem is and see if there is a way you can help them to succeed. If the task is too advanced for them, see if there is a different job they can carry out instead.

Example 1
'John, the bins need to be put outside, you have done that with me many times. I am wondering if you would take responsibility for putting them

outside this week. That would be a great help to the family'.

Example 2

'Ann, I am wondering what jobs you could take responsibility for this week? The dishwasher needs to be emptied and the bathroom sink needs to be cleaned, which would you like to do'?

Example 3

'Pat, the toys need to be tidied away at the end of the day, would you take on doing that for the family, keeping everybody safe'?

The Message the Child Receives

I belong to this family and what I do is helpful. I am able and responsible.

Tip

The chores should be within the child's capabilities. Children should not be paid for everyday family chores like putting their plate in the dishwasher, tidying their rooms or putting their washing in the laundry basket.

This helps to build self-esteem and self-confidence. Remember to acknowledge all efforts.

10 Listening for Feelings

Listen to your child to know and understand their feelings. Remember your child has very little experience in the world and does not understand the feelings they are experiencing. This will help you to form a good relationship with your child. You are trying to understand your child as a person with their own feelings, thoughts and actions. You are building your child's self-esteem and confidence. You are teaching your child emotional intelligence that will serve your child throughout their life.

How to:
Listen to what your child is saying, pick out the feelings behind the words the child is speaking and repeat them back to the child. Check that you have understood what your child is saying with them.

Example 1
Child: 'I hate John.'
Parent: 'It sounds like you are really cross with John.'
Child: 'Yes, I am. He would not play with me at school today.'

Parent: 'It sounds like you felt left out by him and you wanted to play with him.'
Child: 'I did and I had to play all alone.'
Parent: 'It seems like you felt lonely too.'
Example 2
Parent: 'It looks like you are feeling sad.'
Child: 'I am, I miss my cat.'
Parent: 'It seems like you are lonely without your cat.'

The Message the Child Receives
I am loved and understood. What I have to say is important.

Tip
Name your own feelings loudly throughout your day so your child picks up the language of feelings and will learn how to name their own feelings too. 'I feel proud', 'I feel bullied', 'I feel excited.'

11 Listening for Facts

Listen to what your child is actually saying, summarise it and repeat it back to them using some of their words and some of your own. This helps your child to know you have heard them and understand what they are talking about. The parent checks with the child that they have understood correctly. The child learns that what they have to say is important and that what they are doing and saying is important to you. This will help build self-esteem and self-confidence.

How to:
Stop what you are doing, get down to the same level as your child, make eye contact with them and listen to what your child is saying. Repeat what the child says, checking with them that you have understood correctly.

Example 1
John I heard you saying you had no homework this evening and that you want to go out and play.
Example 2
Ann is playing with her dolls and tells you that her baby is sick and needs an injection. You reply by

Saying, 'Oh, your baby is sick and you have to give her an injection so she can get better.'

Example 3

I hear you saying you want to go to the disco tonight, that you will be home before 11 pm and that you can be trusted. You are also telling me that you have not been out since 1 January, is that right?

The Message the Child Receives

I am important, what I have to say is important, my parent understands me and loves me.

Tip

It is important to get down to your child's level, give full attention and eye contact when you are listening, summarising and reflecting back what they say.

12 Spending Time with Your Child

This is a very simple technique but is worth its weight in gold! As parents, we spend a lot of time making sure our children wear warm clothes, eat the right food and put on raincoats when they go out to play but we sometimes forget to spend time enjoying them. It is important because it helps the child to feel valued and it helps build a closer relationship between you, where the child feels they can share with you.

If you master this skill, it will stay with you and your child into adulthood, giving you a close bond and making your child feel like they can come to you with any problem.

How to:
Hang out with your child, looking like you have nothing to do and all day to do it. You are listening to your child, spending time focusing on them and nothing else. You are sharing your thoughts and ideas openly and honestly with your child. You are sharing yourself as a person.

Example 1
When your child comes in from school, stop what you are doing and sit beside them. Ask how their day was and listen intently to what they say. Share similar stories of your childhood with them.

Example 2
Plan an activity with your child and give them your full and undivided attention while you do it. Share your memories relating to that activity with your child and just have fun with them.

Example 3
Sit around in the living room with your children chatting. Look like you have nothing to do, just listen and reflect back what is said. Share your thoughts and stories relating to the conversation.

The Message the Child Receives
I am loved, I am valued and I am fun to be with. My parents like being with me.

Tip
Just 10 to 15 minutes a day giving each child individual attention will make all the difference to them.

13 Being in Your Child's Game

Play is important for children because they learn about the world around them through play. They learn about their feelings and other people's feelings through role play. They learn what it is like to be a mammy, a daddy, a baker, a shopkeeper and so many other roles in the world. It is crucial that you play in your child's games so you can help their learning and understand their thinking. Play helps the child make sense of the world.

How to:
When your child is playing and they ask you to play say 'yes'. Ask your child, in a whisper 'Who do you want me to be in the game'? 'What do you want me to do in the game?' Your child will tell you what to say and do and you do as you are told. During the game ask for more information on how you are to play in a whisper 'Am I doing it right'? If you are doing it right you will be told. You play as you are told. This helps your child to make sense of the thoughts and ideas in their head. In this way you are helping your child's thinking and development in the present moment.

Example 1
Meg and Pam ask a parent to play in their game. They are playing families.
Parent: 'Who do you want me to be in the game?'
Children: 'The baby', neither girl wants to be the baby.
Parent: (whispers) 'What kind of baby am I? Am I a cry baby or a sleepy baby?'
Children: 'A sleepy baby'
Parent: (whispers): 'Do I have a soother?'
Children: 'No, you suck your thumb. You go in the cot over here'
The parent's role in the game is to go to sleep in the cot and suck their thumb.

Example 2
The child is playing with his cars.
Parent: 'May I play'?
Child: 'Yes'.
Parent: 'How would you like me to play'?
Child: 'You use this car and drive along the road there'.
Parent: (whispers): 'How do I drive?'
Child: 'You drive fast and you crash at the end of the road'.
The parent does that.

The Message the Child Receives
My game is fun for my parent. I have fun playing with them.

Tip
Stay in the child's game as much as you can. Your child is gaining insight into the workings of the world, their own feelings and expanding their knowledge and understanding.

14 Acknowledge Effort

It is important to acknowledge your child for the efforts they make to accomplish a task.
Acknowledging effort focusses your child on the value of trying their best and teaches them to enjoy the process. It relieves the pressure of having to be the best at everything or having to win. Your child learns they do not need to win to get your approval, instead they get your encouragement and respect for taking part.

The child can then take part in competitions for enjoyment and have positive feelings about themselves for trying. They learn that winning is part of it but not everything, so they gain a balanced approach to competition.

Example 1
'Well done Ann, you turned up for practice every week and trained hard with your team.'
Example 2
'You worked hard to get your assignment finished and you did your best to make it very interesting for other people.'

Example 3
'You have really succeeded in getting very intense colours in your art work. It was worth all the time you spent mixing the paint to get the tones you wanted. Well done!'

The Message the Child Receives
I am alright taking part and enjoying the activity. I am accepted for trying. Taking part is valued. Doing my best is important.

Tip
Be specific about naming what is good.

15 Healthy Eating

Children need a balanced diet of healthy nutritious food on a daily basis. Your child's behaviour, health and concentration levels are improved by healthy eating habits. The key to a balanced diet is a variety of different foods from the four main food groups of the pyramid. Avoid processed foods as much as possible as natural whole food is best because it provides the nutrition required for energy and growth.

How to:
The food pyramid offers a good guide to the food needs of children.
In the food groups children need:
6 portions /day of potato, rice, cereal, bread, pasta, noodles. (a portion is about the size of a child's fist)
5 portions /day of fruit, vegetables, natural fruit juices.
3 portions /day of cheese, yogurt, milk.
2 portions /day of meat, fish, poultry, eggs, nuts, seeds, peas and beans.
Little to none of oil, butter, cakes, biscuits etc.

Example Day 1
Breakfast: porridge, milk, banana, slice of toast.
Lunch: chicken sandwich, apple, mandarin, water.
Dinner: potato, vegetables, roast meat, stewed apple and milk.
Snacks: popcorn, bread and cheese, water.

Example Day 2
Breakfast: yoghurt, fruit juice, toast and cheese.
Lunch: chicken drumstick, carrots, pasta, water.
Dinner: vegetable and lamb curry, rice, kiwi, water.
Snacks: slice of bread and peanut butter, slice of mango.

Example Day 3
Breakfast: sugar free cereal, milk, bread, natural fruit juice.
Lunch: potato salad, with scrambled egg, blueberries, raspberries.
Dinner: fish, peas, noodles, yogurt, water. Snacks: handful of nuts, coleslaw, cheese square, water.

The Message the Child Receives
Healthy food is tasty and gives me the energy I need to do the activities I want.

Tips
Give your child healthy food from an early age, they will develop a taste for it.

Treats have no nutritional value for your child and can make your child hyper, they should be avoided as much as possible.

Rewarding or bribing your child with treats, will give them an unhealthy relationship with food in their adult lives.

16 Teach Requesting

Teach your young child to request what they want with their words. Throwing tantrums does not help your child to make friends and be accepted by others. Many young children lash out from frustration of not being able to express their needs. If they are taught to request what they want with words, they are able to get along with everyone around them and as a parent you deal with less temper tantrums.

Example 1
'May I play with the lego too?' you say to the child, showing them how to make a request.
Example 2
'May I be your friend and play with you?' the parent says, so Pat can later copy the request.
Example 3
You say to your child: "It sounds like you really want a piece of Jo's cake. You could say to Jo 'Please may I have a piece of your cake' and see what happens." In this way you are teaching the child to ask for what they want.

The Message the Child Receives
Asking for what I want is more effective than throwing tantrums. It is easy to get what I want by asking.

Tip
Teaching your child to request what they want is a lifelong skill. Practice the skill when the child is not upset because it is easier for them to listen and learn. Use this skill to teach your child all the lessons you want them to learn like how to socialise with the people around him, taking turns, saying please and thank you.

17 Children Learn by Doing

Children learn by doing. Remember, they start with knowing little or nothing about the world they are born into. They have so much to learn to be able to take their place in their world as fully functioning adults. It is important to provide material for them to play with safely. Learning is through trial and error. Children do not need expensive toys, with a little creativity, play materials can be free items from everyday life.

How to:
Provide play items that interest the child at different ages. Babies that are under a year old need items to mouth. Toddlers need items to wheel, carry and fit into each other. Each child has special interests, you need to pay attention to what your child is interested in and find items that further their interest.

Example 1
The items you provide can be homemade. They can be things in your house, in your garden or from the environment around you. Sand, water, sticks, stones, cones, shells, grass, leaves, pipes,

boxes, buckets, containers are all examples of free materials that can provide hours of fun for children. Collect enough material so that they can use it in many different ways.

Example 2

Children love to copy what they see around them so provide items that are used by adults, like a 'housekeeper's kit' with a sweeping brush, a mop, cut down to a child's size, a dust pan and brush. A shoe polish set with a brush, a small shoe and cloths for shining shoes.

A 'hair dressers box' could include an old hair dryer - with the cord removed for safety - a brush, comb and rollers.

A 'makeup box', an 'office box' and a 'tool box' are other sets that can be made up for children with just a little thought and very little cash.

Example 3

Regular toys are also a good way for children to learn. These can be new or second hand.

Example 4

Outings are a great way to help the child's learning, usually children enjoy mimicking what their parents do.

The Message the Child Receives
Learning is fun and I am able.

Tip

Observe what your child is interested in, include items of interest to them in their playthings. For example, if your child loves arts and crafts, collect materials to encourage that interest.

Remember, you do not have to spend lots of money to provide toys for children - they are often more interested in the wrapping paper and boxes that toys come in!

18 Teach Feeling Language

Teaching your child the language of feelings is very important. The child becomes aware of their feelings about themselves and other people. They can communicate their feelings more easily, learn to take steps to sort out their emotional problems.

How to:
 The first step is for parents to tune into their own feelings and start to name them out loud so the child becomes aware of them. The parent needs to pick out the child's feelings and name them too.

Examples
'Jan you felt hurt inside when your friend would not play with you'
'Sam you felt angry with Jo for taking your toy'
'You feel jealous of Pat because he has a new bicycle'
'You felt happy when Mary came to play with you'
'Ben you felt sad when your dad did not come to collect you'
'You felt proud when you won a gold star today'
'You felt bullied when Pat took your pencils again today'

The Message the Child Receives
I am understood, I am accepted and I am loved

Tips
All feelings are acceptable positive and negative. Avoid judging the feelings as bad or good. Just acknowledge the child's feelings as they arise. It is one of the greatest skills you can teach your child.

19 Giving Your Child Attention

It is important to give your child positive attention on a regular basis. Children are looking for the attention of the important adults in their lives, to feel loved, accepted, cared for and recognised as worthwhile human beings. Your child needs your attention on an ongoing basis. If the child does not receive attention through positive behaviour, the child will turn to negative behaviour and gain your attention this way.

Example 1
'Hey Sam you have really worked hard at putting that jigsaw together. How did you do it?' Wait and listen to what the child has to say and repeat what he says to check in that you have got it right. He knows you have heard him.

Example 2
'I am wondering if it is a good idea to eat lunch outside today and how can we do it easily. What do you think Tom?' Listen to what he has to say and then do it together.

Example 3
You found a way to do that chore easily how did you think of that? Wait and listen to the answer.

The Message the Child Receives
What I think is important, what I do is important, I am important in this family.

Tips
You are sharing control of family life with your children. They help to make small family decisions. You show interest in what they are doing and thinking and so build their self-esteem and self-confidence.

20 Learning Decision Making

Decisions are part of everyone's life. My youngest daughter struggled with getting dressed every morning. Soon I realised it was that she could not choose what to wear. This knowledge completely changed our mornings. I laid out two outfits for her to choose from. She was dressed in five minutes after that.

Children need to learn to make their own decisions, with parents help. Start off when they are young. Give a young child simple decisions to make - an either / or decision. As they get older they are able to make a choice between more than two things. In this way they do not get overwhelmed with choices.

Example 1
'You can either have sausage and potato or egg and potato, which do you want?'
Example 2
'You can either wear this outfit or that outfit, which do you want to wear?

Example 3

'It is bedtime, you can either walk up to your bed or I will carry you up. Which do you want to do?'

The Message the Child Receives

I can choose for myself. I have control over my life, I am important and respected in my family. My family love me.

Tip

Children feel control over areas of their lives on a daily basis and do not have to fight with their parents for control.

21 Planning as a Family

Weekly family planning meetings are important to discuss outings, chores, complaints and future family plans. Family meetings are about sharing control in the home with your children. Giving the children some say in family events, family life.

How to:
Hold your family meeting weekly after dinner or a time when everyone is around and at leisure.
Plan outings and chores at these meetings. Ensure that outing destination suggestions are considered from every member of the family. Create an agenda where all the family have a say. Avoid family meetings being about chores only. Ensure fun activities are planned too. Have some simple rules about meetings. For example one person speaks at a time, everyone gets an opportunity to speak and be heard.

Example
'On the agenda today we have our visit to the zoo next month. We need to plan what we are bringing with us and who is in charge of each thing we need. The family chores for this coming week need to be discussed. We need to look at

all the good things that have happened with the family in the week gone by and so on.

The Message the Child Receives
I am an important part of this family, the things I do help this family, I have choices in this family

Tips
Begin the meeting with naming all the good things that happened in the family the week before. Sandwich the chores between fun things, make sure there are fun things and chores for meetings. Otherwise children will be slow to engage in meetings.

22 Community Involvement

It is important for the child's development as they get older that they are involved in the community. For the first few years the home is their whole world but as they get older they need opportunities to practise their social skills in order to learn to make friends and build relationships outside the family. Being involved in the community helps children gain a sense of belonging, which is important as they grow up.

As a parent, it is also important for you to be involved in the community, leading by example for your children.

Example 1
Take part in community sport, athletics, boxing, yoga, dancing or whatever activity your child is interested in. Children are often interested in the same activities as their parents.

Example 2
Involvement in the local drama club, writer's group, beekeeping group or musical society, are all community activities where children can learn valuable skills about being part of a community.

Example 3
Volunteering at events as a family, like baking for community functions or being involved in a town clean-up allows children to bond with their family while contributing to the community.

The Message the Child Receives
I am part of this community. I belong here. I am accepted and my family are accepted here.

Tip
Children need lots of opportunities to practise their social skills. Teach your child how to meet and greet people, how to behave in social settings so they feel comfortable in social gatherings.

23 Parent Self-Care

A vital part of meeting children's needs is that parents care for themselves and are physically and emotionally able to parent. The parent who looks after themselves is less likely to be stressed, is more tolerant and has more energy for their children. They have a balance between their own needs and the needs of their children.

Examples of Activities for Parents
- Playing a sport and keeping fit is important for physical health and mental well-being.

- Meditation, tai chi, yoga or any calming activity allows you to relax and have some 'me time'.

- Spending time socialising with friends and family or involvement in local activities are important so that you do not feel like your identity is solely linked to your role as a parent.

- Create support systems around the family, for example, having babysitters organised on a weekly or bi-monthly basis or having a back-up plan for someone to collect or mind the children if you are sick or running late.

- Eating nutritious healthy meals will help parents to feel better and have more energy.

- Getting enough sleep at night is important.

Part 2

24 Your Child is Separate from Your Child's Behaviour

It is important to separate your child from their behaviour. Your child is not their behaviour. You may not always agree with their behaviour or their actions but no matter what, you will always love your child.

How to:
It's like a sandwich. You reinforce your love for your child, you name the behaviour you do not like, give a clear description of the behaviour you expect.

Example 1
'John I love you dearly but I do not like the way you speak to your sister. I want you to talk to her in a calm voice'.
Example 2
'Ann I love you, but I do not like the way you leave your dishes all over the sitting room. I want you to leave your dishes on the sink after you eat'.

Example 3
'Pat I really love you, I do not like how you leave your books on the kitchen table after you do your homework. I want you to put them in your bag and put your bag under the stairs as soon as you have finished'.

The Message the Child Receives
I am loved but my behaviour is not acceptable.

Tip
If your child ignores you, you follow up with action. Change the way things happen or look at the consequence pages.

25 Misbehaving and What the Child Gains

Children misbehave if there is something to gain from it. A guide to help you to know what is happening is to pay attention to your own feelings.

Here are some reasons children misbehave:
1. To gain power, security and control over circumstances - which may make you the parent feel angry or bullied.
2. To get attention – You the parent may feel irritated.
3. To show off to other children who are around so as to get attention from them - You may feel irritated and afraid for your child.
4. To get revenge for past slights or hurts - You may feel hurt, sad, disappointed.
5. To get other people to do things for them - You may feel impatient with the child.
6. Doing dangerous things for attention. You may feel afraid for your child.

Example 1: Power
John is asked to do his homework. He shouts 'No, I will not do my homework and you can't make me'.

Example 2: Attention
Ali breaks his sister's toy, she gives out to him. Ali goes to the parent crying.

Example 3: Revenge
Ann thinks, 'I will throw the ornaments on the floor and that will teach her to give me the toy when I ask'.

Example 4: Status
'I hate this awful food' John says looking for a reaction from his friends. His friends laugh.

Example 5: Service
'I can't finish my homework and teacher will be cross with me if I haven't it done, will you do it for me?' said in a helpless voice.

26 Natural Consequences

Natural consequences are the outcomes of an action taken. If I go to work without my lunch, I will be hungry. This is the automatic result of my action or lack of care for myself. Children need to learn from natural consequences existing in the environment they live in. Parents who understand consequences and their use will avoid arguments with their children in situations where the child does not want to do as they are requested.

Example 1
Sam insists on wearing no gloves building a snowman, he gets cold fingers, cold hands and he feels the pain of the cold. Sam gains first-hand experience of the result of not wearing gloves. The next time Sam will know to wear his gloves.
Example 2
John hits his friend Pat while playing, Pat does not want to play with John anymore. John learns that hitting his friend, loses his friend.
Example 3
Ann insists on wearing snow boots in summer, her feet get very hot and sweaty and she feels very

uncomfortable. She learns that snow boots are not worn in summer because they are too warm.

Example 4

Cara hugs her younger brother Matt. Matt later comes and kisses her. Cara learns that being gentle and loving gets her positive attention.

The Message the Child Receives

I can learn by myself. I know myself. I can make decisions for myself.

Tip

While still keeping your child safe, do not rescue, or interfere with the child's choice. Let the child feel the full impact of the action taken. Otherwise, the child does not learn.

27 Logical Consequences

Some actions have no natural consequences so the child does not learn that their behaviour is not acceptable. In this case the parent decides on a logical consequence for the child's behaviour. The consequence needs to be connected to the behaviour. The parent explains the consequence of a behaviour to the child and if the child doesn't listen the parent must follow through on the consequence.

Example 1
Jo breaks his toy on purpose. He asks his parent to buy him a new toy. The parent refuses to buy Jo a new toy. Jo learns that breaking the toy means he has lost the toy.

Example 2
Ahmed steals a toy from a shop. The parent insists Ahmed brings back the toy to the shop and apologises to the manager in the shop. Ahmed learns that stealing is wrong.

Example 3
Sarah refuses to stay with her parent when they go to the supermarket. She constantly wanders off. The parent tells her that if she wanders off in

the supermarket again she will be brought straight home and will miss out on the next shopping outing. Mum carries through on her words.

Example 4

The child does not go to bed at bedtime. The following night bedtime is fifteen minutes earlier. The parent ensures that this happens by starting the bedtime routine earlier. Give the child the choice at bedtime of how they are going up to bed. The bedtime is not the child's decision. 'You can walk up or I can carry you up to bed, which do you want to do? Give the child the choice of how they are going to bed not the time they are going to bed. Carry them up to bed calmly and firmly if no decision has been made.

The Message the Child Receives

I have choices and what I choose has results for me. I can manage my life.

Tip

Let the child feel the result of their actions. Consequences need to be related to the behaviour so the child can connect the behaviour to the consequence.

28 Problem Solving With the Young Child

Problem solving is a skill that can be used at every stage of growing up. When children are young it can be used to sort out fights over toys, arguments over chores and fallings out with friends. It is a skill that takes a bit of time to implement but it is a skill for life. The parent is trying to create a win-win result for each child. As children become skilled at the technique it takes less time to implement. After some time children are able to sort out their problems themselves.

How to:
- Stop children from hitting and hurting each other while staying calm and unbiased.
- You take the toy they are fighting over and hold onto it.
- Name each child's feelings until they calm down.
- Ask each child what has happened, listen to what each one says and repeat it back for the other child to hear.

- Say 'you have a problem'. 'You both want the toy at the same time'.
- Ask how the children are going to sort out their problem.
- Listen to each one's solution, repeat it and check if the suggestion is acceptable to the other child.
- If it is, then that is the solution.
- If it is not acceptable the process continues until a solution is reached that the two children agree on.
- You may suggest solutions if the children cannot.
- Double check that they both agree to the solution.
- When they do agree on a solution, follow up afterwards and make sure the agreement is kept or start the process again.

Example 1
Sal and Jack are fighting over a shovel. Sal is hitting Jack with the shovel. The parent calmly takes the shovel from Sal.
Parent: 'I am holding onto this shovel until we sort out the problem'.

Parent: 'You are feeling hurt Jack, you are feeling angry Sal. It sounds like you are both really cross with each other.'
Parent: 'What happened Sal?'
Sal: 'Jack took my shovel'.
Parent: 'Sal says you took his shovel'
Jack: 'He hit me with the shovel, it's my shovel'.
Parent: 'Jack says you hit him with the shovel and it is his shovel.'
Sal says: 'I want that shovel.'
Parent: 'Sal says that he wants the shovel.'
Jack: 'I had it first'.
Parent: 'Jack says he had it first.'
Parent: 'It sounds like you both want the same shovel. How can you sort out this problem?'. Jack suggests: 'I will have it first and then he will have it'.
Sal replies: 'No, I want it now. I will give it to him in ten minutes when I have finished.'
Jack: 'No, I was using it.'
Parent: 'There is another shovel in the sand outside, maybe one of you could play with that'.
Sal: 'I want that shovel,' he runs off to get it.

Example 2

Maria and Jason are fighting over the front seat of the car, pushing each other out of the way. The parent locks the car doors and says: 'It looks like you are both cross with each other and you both want the front seat of the car. You need to sort this problem before we go out.'

Maria: 'I am the oldest I should have the front seat.'

Jason: 'I want to sit in the front seat, I always have to sit in the back, It is not fair.'

Parent: 'It looks like Maria you think being the oldest, you should have the front seat and, Jason, you are feeling unfairly treated because you always have to sit in the back seat. How do you think you are going to solve this problem? We only have one front seat.'

Maria: 'He can sit in the back.'

Jason; 'No it's not fair.'

Parent: 'It looks like that is not a solution. Is there any other solution you can think of that would work for both of you?'

Jason: 'I could sit in the front seat on the journey going out and Maria could sit in the front seat on the return journey.'

Maria; 'That's ok with me.'

Parent: 'Well done, you have the problem sorted.'

The Message the Child Receives

I am able to sort out my own problems.

Tip

Make sure that both children agree with the solution. Otherwise, it is not a solution. Follow up on any agreement they make and make sure it happens. Otherwise they will not believe you the next time. The solution has to be their solution.

29 Problem Solving for the Older Child

The technique needs to be adapted for the older child and the teenager. It is a life skill and helps children to look at every possible option to a solution. Children learn to explore different options. It is useful when problems are outside the family.

How to:
Listen to your child, then pick out the feelings they are experiencing and reflect them back, checking that you have understood them. Listen further, until your child has expressed everything about the problem. Ask your child what they could do to solve the problem. Write down all the solutions you and your child come up with, no matter how silly they are. Go back over each one asking what the child thinks might happen if they used that solution. If the child does not like the outcome to the solution then that solution is dropped until there are two to three solutions left. Ask the child which solution they would like to try first.
Decide on when the solution will be carried out.

Plan to chat about the outcome the next evening. If the problem has not been sorted then look at the next favourite solution on the list. And make a plan to carry out that solution. Work through the solutions until the problem is sorted out.

Example 1
Jane comes home from school saying her best friend Mary said she did not want to be her friend anymore. Mary has found a new friend Sue who is excluding Jane. Parent: 'It sounds like you feel hurt inside by Mary, rejected, all alone as she does not want to be your friend anymore.'
Jane: 'I do, we have been friends for years and now she does not answer my texts or talk to me. She talks to Sue all the time.'
Parent: 'That sounds like you are feeling really hurt and left out.'
Jane: 'I do not know what to do about it.'
Parent: 'Is there anything you can think of that might work?'
Jane: 'I could call around to her house and ask her why she is not my friend anymore,' 'I could ask her at school tomorrow, I could make friends with Patsy and not be her friend at all,'
Parent: 'Is there anything else you could do?'
Jane: 'I could try to be friends with Sue.'

Parent: 'Let's look at what would happen if you called around to her house and asked why she is not your friend anymore.'

Jane; 'She would ask me in and we would talk or she could close the door on me.'

Parent: 'How would that be for you?'

Jane; 'I would feel awful.'

Parent: 'What would happen if you asked her at school tomorrow?'

Jane: 'She might talk to me if I got her on her own.'

Parent: 'What about making friends with Patsy?'

Jane: 'That would not be the same but it might be alright.'

Parent: What would it be like to make friends with Sue?'

Jane: 'I do not like her, she says mean things about people.'

Parent: 'So what do you think you will try first?'

Jane: 'I will try to talk to Mary on her own in school and maybe I could start to be friends with Patsy more.'

Parent: 'When will you do that?'

Jane: 'Tomorrow at school.'

Parent: 'We will talk again tomorrow evening and see how it goes.'

Example 2

Jane says that her teacher is always giving out to her and never gives out to the other girls in class.

Parent: 'You feel picked on and unfairly treated by your teacher.'

Jane: 'Yes, I think my teacher does not like me. She speaks to me sharply.'

Parent: 'You feel disliked by your teacher. So what do you think you could do about it?'

Jane: 'I could make sure to have my homework done, I could stop talking in class or you could go in and talk to her for me.'

Parent: 'Anything else you could do?'

Jane 'No.'

Parent 'What do you think would happen if you had your homework done and stopped talking in class?'

Jane: 'That might work.'

Parent: 'What do you think would happen if I went in to talk to your teacher?'

Jane: 'It might sort the problem or it might make it worse.'

Parent: 'Which solution would you like to try first?'

Jane: 'I will stop talking and have my homework done for the next three days. If that does not work, will you go and talk to her?'

Parent: 'That sounds like a plan, we will talk over the next three days again.'

The Message the Child Receives
I have control over my life. I am able to sort out my problems. My mum trusts and supports me.

Tip
Make sure to check in with the child, see what has worked and what has not and problem solve until there is a resolution.

30 When and....Then

When and....Then is a very simple technique. It is used to get activities and jobs done children do not like doing without a fuss, that are part of life.

How to:
The parent says to the child when you have done task A, we can do activity B. The task is followed by something the child likes. The child has an incentive to complete the task and get the reward.

Example 1
John hates doing his homework. Mam says 'John when you have done your homework we will have dinner.'
Example 2
'We will go shopping when you put away your toys.'
Example 3
'You can go out and play when you have changed your uniform.'

The Message the Child Receives
I must change my uniform quickly to get out to play quickly. I must keep my uniform clean.

Tip

There are chores that need to be done that the child does not like doing, if the chore is followed up by something the child enjoys, it makes it easier for the child and the parent.

31 Feeling.. Limit.. Another Action

This technique is used when the child does not want to do something that needs to be done in the moment or when the child gets angry and is about to express his feeling physically.

How to:
The parent names the child's feeling, reminds the child of the rule or limit and suggests another action to the child.

Example 1
I know you are feeling angry with your sister for taking your toy. It is not allowed to hit your sister, you can hit the teddy bear instead.

Example 2
It is time to go to collect your brother at the school. I know you feel frustrated to leave your game, you can bring your game with you and continue to play.

Example 3
I know you feel hurt because your friend won't play with you. It is not allowed to tear her book. You can tear the newspaper over there instead.

The Message the Child Receives
The child learns there are limitations to be kept and choices to make about behaviour.

Tip
This technique is useful when the child is about to break a rule, it is prevention.

32 Requesting a Change of Behaviour from Your Child

You use this requesting technique when you want to request a change of behaviour from your child without blaming your child or having your child feel belittled or diminished.

How to:
State what you feel about the behaviour, name the behaviour, and request the behaviour you would like instead.

Example 1
'John I feel hurt inside when you shout at me when I ask you to do something. I want you to answer me in a calm voice'.

Example 2
'I feel annoyed when you leave your toys thrown all over the kitchen floor. I want you to put away your toys when you are finished with them.'

Example 3
'I feel used when you leave your dishes on the table. I want you to put your dishes in the sink after you have finished your meals.'

The Message the Child Receives
My mum treats me well, she has asked me to help her.

Tip
Do not continue requesting the same thing. The child has heard you and chosen to ignore you. The parent needs to follow up with an action or a consequence.

33 Children's Asking Styles

Children try to get their needs met in many ways. They quickly tune in to the asking styles that get them what they want. Often, we, as parents are unaware of their asking styles. The key thing for the parent is to know that it is just the way the child has learned to get their needs met. The parent needs to stick to what they have said. 'No' means 'No' and stay calm. Do not let the boundaries move. Give your explanation once and stick to your guns. Children will use a combination of these techniques at any one time to get their needs met.

Example 1-'Begging Benny'
'Please, please, please Mam, I beg you Mam, I want….' or 'I beg you, beg you, can I have.' or words of that kind.

Example 2 'Constant Connie'
'I want a new bicycle, I want a new bicycle, I want a new bicycle' repeated at every opportunity every day until it is gotten. Then there is usually something else wanted.

Example 3 'Lovely Lily'
'You are the best mam ever, I love you to bits always, yummy mummy, the kindest mum ever' or something similar. I want.....

Example 4 'Heart Felt Harry'
'Mam If you do not let me go to Jane's party I will be left out tomorrow, no one will talk to me and I will have no friends to talk to. They will all be talking about the party.
Or
'I have to have the 'designer' top, I will be the only one with no top and I will have no friends'. I need

Example 5 'Billy Bluff '
'If you don't let me do that I will ring 'child line' and then you will be in trouble'
Or
'I will run away from home if you do not do what I ask'.

Example 6 'Tommy Tantrum'
'You never let me do anything I want' shouts the child as they turn and walk out the door, slamming it, turning and kicking it.
Or
The child lies down on the floor kicking and screaming to get what she wants in the shop.

Or
The child shouts, screams at the dad throwing furniture on the ground because dad will not let their friend come over to visit as it is very late.

34 'Time Out'

'Time out' is a technique where the child is withdrawn from the company of others to help the child calm down and reflect on what is happening. A short period of time away from the situation that is frustrating a child is used with young children and with older children. Young children benefit from time out from fighting with their siblings. Time out can be supported by the presence of a parent for younger and older children. Time out needs to be discussed with children in advance of applying it.

Example 1
'John, I can see you are really frustrated with your brother. You need to come away and sit in the kitchen here, calm down and think about what is happening between you.'

Example 2
'Sarah, if you continue arguing with me you are going to be on time out. If you have not changed your behaviour on the count of three you are on time out for the next five minutes.'

Example 3
'Treating your brother with respect is important in this family. If, on the count of three, you have not

started to treat your brother with respect you are on 'Time out' for ten minutes to reflect on ways of treating your brother more respectfully.'

The Message the Child Receives
I need to think about changing my behaviour or their will be consequences. My behaviour is not acceptable

Tips
It is important that when a parent uses 'Time out', they follow through removing the child from the company or situation the child is in. It is important that 'Time out' begins when the child is removed from the company of other family members, friends, from where the difficulty is occurring.

35 Self-Defence Parenting

It happens that a child is hitting her parent and the parent does not know how to deal with this situation. It happens that a child is breaking things in the family home. The parent needs to immediately stop this behaviour. It is a way to get what the child wants or vent frustration. If the child sees that it works for them the child will continue with this behaviour. It is much easier to stop the hitting as soon as it starts otherwise it becomes an acceptable habit.

How to:
The parent needs to say 'Stop!!! Do not hit me!!! I do not like it' in a loud strong voice that the child is not used to, as soon as the child begins to hit the parent. It is no good saying it in your usual calm voice. It needs to be said forcefully so the child gets the message loud and clear that it is not acceptable behaviour.

If you have to stop your child physically hitting you, do so. You are stronger. Then walk away. Give no more attention than is necessary to deal with the situation. Remove yourself from your child to let both of you calm down. Pay attention to what your child is looking for from this behaviour. When you have both calmed down later, talk to your child, listen to what they are saying. Remind your child that hitting you will never get what the child is looking for. Review the chapters on 'Decision Making' and 'What My Child Gains from Misbehaving' again.

Example 1
John has started hitting his mum he wants a new Ipod and mum has refused to get it for him.
Mum: 'Stop!!! don't do that!!! I don't like it,' in a very loud, strong, forceful voice.
'It will get you nothing,' mum walks away giving no more attention.
Example 2
Amy has started throwing the furniture on the floor.
Mum: 'I can see you are very angry. It is not allowed to break the furniture. Go and punch the couch instead,'

The Message the Child Receives
It is not ok to hit mum. I will not get what I want this way.

Tip

Stop your child hitting you as soon as it starts otherwise the problem will continue to escalate. It is not acceptable behaviour.

36 Building Self-Esteem Tips.

All of the techniques covered will help your child grow in self-confidence and self-esteem. Here are some additional ones.

- Show your child you love and accept them exactly as they are.

- Copy your child, mirror what your child is doing. If you copy your child's actions, the child gets the message, 'what I am doing is alright' It helps to build good self-esteem.

- Keep calm and speak to your child like you would your friend.

- Be the role model for your child, your child will do as you do not as you say.

- Give your child just enough help to do a task he is not able to do, no more than is needed for him to succeed.

- Name the behaviour you like that your child does so he is clear of your expectations. Ignore behaviours you do not want your child repeating.

- Know your child's capabilities and do not expect too much or too little from your child.

- Remember you are the parent, your job is to lead in the family often making unpopular decisions that your children resist.

- Observe your child, it will help you to know your child. Keep a diary for your child.

- Keep a note of your child's likes, dislikes, interests and skills.

- Give your child your undivided attention for at least ten minutes a day where you put down what you are doing and focus totally on your child.

- Remember you are the best parent you can be at this moment in time.

- Avoid comparing your children with each other or comparing your child to other children. Each child is unique and acceptable the way they are.

- When you are wrong, own it and apologise to your child.

- Help your child to understand mistakes are opportunities to grow and learn new things.

- Help your child discover their uniqueness, their talents and ambitions by pointing them out and naming them.

- Try to meet as many needs of your child as you can.

- You are your child's most important asset. Your child wants to spend their time with you. Believe it or not you are 'God' in their life. They do not care how much money you have or have not.

- Create time to spend with your children having fun, daily if you can, at least weekly.

- Avoid criticisms, comparisons or smart remarks, your child gets deeply hurt by them.

- Never do anything for your child that the child is able to do for themselves.

37 Reducing Conflict at Home

- Make sure children have enough sleep at night and are not cranky during the day.

- Feed children before they are hungry.

- Remove all distractions before doing homework.

- Boredom causes conflict. Create and manage interesting activities for children.

- Check if the child is sick as this can lead to conflicts. The child can be contrary, upset and not able to deal with simple frustrations that would be easily dealt with if the child was well.

- Set out clear expectations of behaviour, name the behaviour you want exactly.

- Go down to the child's level to give clear instructions.

- Give young children one instruction at a time.

- Make sure everybody is clear on the house rules.

- Consistently keep the boundaries you create in the family. Keep the family rules at all times.

- Watch out for triggers to behaviours and avoid them.

- Follow through on consequences for bad behaviour immediately, state the request or limit one time and then act. Your child has heard you and chosen to ignore you.

- Give children warnings before changes occur. 'We will be going to the school in 10 minutes'. We will be leaving in 2 minutes. This gives the child the chance to bring their activity to a natural conclusion.

- Avoid blaming your child unfairly. Gather all the facts about the situation that arises.

- Shrugging is a technique to use to avoid conflict when the child is using threats.

- Do not react to what is said in anger.

- Ensure children get lots of opportunities to make decisions.

- Do the unexpected sometimes. If you are normally loud, be quiet, If you normally nag, find something to encourage. If you normally give attention, give no attention.

- Look after yourself, do something you like doing. A happy parent gets a happy child.

- When there is a conflict between you and the child, pay attention to what happens before the conflict, what happens during the conflict and after the conflict. Write it down, watch the pattern. This will help you to make more informed decisions about resolving the conflict.

- Look to see what a child gains from misbehaving.

- Give lots of attention for positive behaviour when the child is not looking for attention.

- Enjoy your child. These are precious years. All too soon they will have grown up, living their own lives.

Part 3
Difficulties Experienced by Parents

My child will not go to bed at bedtime. What should I do?

Set a bed time rule in your home with your child, make sure the child knows the rule or is involved in creating the rule. Look at the section on 'House Rules'. Give time warnings to your child. 'It's fifteen minutes before bedtime.' 'It's five minutes before bedtime.' 'It's now bedtime.' 'Do you want to walk up to bed or be carried up to bed?' The bedtime is not negotiable but the way you go to bed is. The child is given control over how they are going to bed, not the bedtime.

If there are rituals before bedtime like a story time, washing teeth time, bath time, it is done in the same way. 'It's story time, do you want me to pick the story or do you want to pick your story?' 'It is bath time, do you want me to shampoo your hair or do you want to do it yourself?'

My child is throwing tantrums when he does not get what he wants. He shouts and gives out. He throws things about. What should I do?

He has learnt that throwing a tantrum gets him what he wants. It works for him. He will not stop until it does not work for him anymore. Explain to him the rules of the house when he is calm. Remind him 'It's not allowed to break things in the house.' Remove your valuables until this time has passed. Read the page on 'A Hundred Hugs a Day', giving him lots of attention when he is not looking for it. Read the page on 'Learning Decision Making', incorporating more choices in your child's day giving him more power and control in his life. Review the 'Children's Asking Styles' section and the 'Logical Consequences' section. Decide on a consequence for his behaviour, explain the consequence of his actions and carry through on the consequence consistently at the moment of the tantrums. The child connects the consequence to the behaviour if it is carried out immediately. Acknowledge your child for requesting what he wants on an ongoing basis.

My child is fearful. She is afraid to go to bed at night. What can I do?

Review the 'Listening for Feelings' section of this book. Try to work out what she is afraid of exactly. 'Listen for Facts'. Review the 'Problem Solving' section. Problem solve with her ways to help her feel safer when going to bed. Decide a plan of action with her. Talk to her about fears being natural and that we all have fears. Reassure her. Give her a soft toy to sleep with, an item of your clothing, or play a recording of your voice before sleeping, maybe telling a story to help her sleep.

My child insists on being on his iPad for hours. I don't think it is good for him. What can I do?

Decide exactly what you think is the right amount of time for him to be on his iPad. Talk to your child about your concerns and your wishes. Listen to what your child is saying. Make a decision from the information you have on how long your child should be on the iPad. Communicate this to your child. If you decide the week end is the time for the iPad then put it away until the weekend. If the child breaks the new rule, review the 'Logical Consequences' section. Decide on the consequences with the child. Ensure the child knows the consequence and then you consistently carry through with the consequence. A consequence may be that he misses a turn on the iPad.

My child constantly whinges for what they want. What can I do about it?

Your child has learnt that this way works for them. They get exactly what they want when they whinge. Your job is to teach them new ways of asking. Look at the page on 'Teach Requesting'. Teach them how to request what they want. Acknowledge your child every time they use the new requesting style and do not respond to the whinging for things. Persevere and you will soon see changes.

My child has started hitting me when I do not do what they ask. They throw things around and break them. What can I do?

Speak to your child about the 'no hitting rule' in your 'House Rules' in a firm clear voice when things are calm. Clear away everything you value that is breakable from the room you are in before the next outburst happens. If your child continues to hit you, in a very loud, firm tone of voice tell your child to stop hitting you.
'Stop! Don't do that. I don't like it, hitting is not allowed in this house'. Make it perfectly clear it is not acceptable behaviour with a strong voice. Block your child from hitting you if that is necessary. You are physically stronger. Walk away from your child giving your child no attention for his or her behaviour. Remain calm while this happens.

This behaviour needs to be stopped at a young age so that it does not continue on into later years, when your child will grow stronger. Remember this is a strategy your child uses to get what they want, to vent frustration or to get attention. Review the section on 'Misbehaving and What the Child Gains'. It is probably power the child is looking for. Make sure the child never gets the result they are expecting from this behaviour. The child continues this behaviour because at some level it works for them.

Look at the 'Learning Decision Making' section, see where your child can gain more choices over their life. Your child may need more control over their life. You may need to give them more choices.

If it is your attention they are seeking, give none at this moment in time. Review the 'Hundred Hugs a Day' section to increase the positive attention your child receives when not looking for it, reducing their need to seek out negative attention.

Review the 'Listening to Understand & Listening for Feelings' sections. At a different time ask your child what is happening for them. Listen and reflect back their feelings.

My youngest child keeps hitting his sibling. What can I do to stop this happening?

Talk to your child about the 'no hitting rule' in the 'House Rules' section at a calm moment. Act immediately when the behaviour starts happening. Stop the hitting. Listen to what the child says about the hitting of his sibling. Listen to the older child and what they are saying. Look at the sections on 'Listening for Feelings & Listening for Facts'. The 'Problem Solving' section will also help to sort out rows over toys. Everything in Part One of the book applies.

My child refuses to do any household chores. What can I do?

Talk with your child, listen to understand. Maybe your child sees the chore they have as not being important, not contributing to the family. Check and see if there is another chore they like to do. Remind your child that everybody is doing chores to create a better family life. Explain to your child how the family works and everybody's role in the family working together. Support your child in carrying out whatever chore they agree to. Acknowledge them for their contribution to the family regularly and point out the benefits the family get from them doing their chores.

My child is very shy. How can I help them?

Some children are shyer and quieter than others. If being shy is a difficulty for your child use all of the techniques in Part One and the self-esteem building tips in Part Two. This will help to build up your child's confidence. Talk to your child about shyness in an exploring way, look it up on the internet together. Learn as much as you can about it with your child if they are willing to. Problem solve together. Role play with your child situations your child finds difficult.

My child is being bullied at school. What can I do?

Bullying is one thing adults cannot ignore. Your child does not have the skills needed to tackle this problem. You, the adult need to get to the source of the bullying and put steps in place to stop it. If the bullying happens at school you need to speak to the teacher and the principal. If it is outside of school you need to speak to the parents of the other child and sort it out.

All of Part One will help you to build your child's self-esteem and confidence again. If your child is being bullied by a child the same age look at the 'Problem Solving' page and help your child to find ways to solve the problem.

My child is the bully at school. What can I do about it?

Your child is loudly saying that all is not well in their world. You need to listen to what your child is saying and find out what is happening for your child. The 'Listening for Feelings' and 'Listening for Facts' and all of Part One is relevant to you. Read it again and start to put some of the methods into practice. The section on listening to your child, particularly 'Listening for Feelings' is very useful for you to work out what is happening for your child.

This way you get to the root of the problem. Your child feels heard. You can then read the 'Problem Solving' section and help your child sort out his difficulties. Your child needs your help dealing with feelings and emotions. Start to name emotions on a daily basis for your child. Talk about your own emotions.

My child is tearful all the time. What can I do?

If your child is tearful all the time something is not working in their world. You need to listen to understand what is happening for them. Read the 'Listening for Feelings' and 'Listening for Facts' pages to help you get to the bottom of the problem. Be alert for unusual behaviour. Read all of Part One it will help you to support your child through this tough time.

Conclusion

Parenting is a difficult job with little or no training or support for parents. The techniques in this book will help new parents early on in their parenting to build up ways of being positive with their children. Parents will be helped to build strong relationships with their children that will last throughout the growing up years into adulthood and foster healthy lifelong communication skills.

This book will reaffirm the parenting skills of existing parents. Many parents worry if they are 'doing it right.' Nobody tells them they are doing a good job. Most parents are doing the best they possibly can to have their children grow up happy and healthy. Parents need to be acknowledged and supported for the huge job they do rearing the next generation, especially considering the huge technological changes that have taken place since they were children themselves.

The techniques covered in Part One are mainly preventative, outlining ways of building a strong relationship with your child. It is crucial that parents read Part One over and over again, applying the techniques consistently until they become second nature. We are all inclined to forget things.

Part One focuses the parent on the needs of children, the need for showing your child unconditional love. It teaches the importance of being with your child through play, through listening and of reflecting back to your child. General routine, health, safety, house rules, parent care are also dealt with as really important issues for children and parents. The idea is that the more of the bonding exercises you practise such as building self-esteem and self-confidence in Part One, the less need you will have for Part Two.

Part Two should be used when families have difficulty with the behaviour of children. Difficult behaviours are part of family life, it is normal. Children change as they grow, going through many stages towards independence. Parents have to adapt their techniques to accommodate the growing child. There are different techniques that can be used in different situations. By combining them, most difficulties can be solved. Many of the techniques are life skills that children will use to build better relationships in their own lives. Again, they are skills that can be passed on from generation to generation, building a better quality of life for each generation. The skills you use parenting your child will prepare your child to rear your grandchildren into being healthy, emotionally mature adults.

Part three covers common difficulties parents experience rearing their children. Each question refers the reader back to sections in the book to help them to solve the difficulties they are experiencing. Part One of the book is helpful in every case that arises.

Finally, the author would like that this book enables parents worldwide to be competent, calm, relaxed and skilled parents, connecting families with bonds made of steel.

Thank you for reading my book

Grainne Brady

www.childknowhow.com

Made in the USA
Columbia, SC
05 April 2018